Contents

By reading this manual you will have more knowledge of how to understand and measure body composition.

This is useful for nutritionists, fitness and sports coaches and individuals interested in improving health.

Body fat measurement is an important indicator of not only fitness level but also a predictor of future health risks.

A person's weight does not give a clear indication of the health of that individual. Body weight alone does not take into account the composition of a person in terms of lean body mass (muscle) versus fat mass.

Ideal body composition should be a lifelong goal

Methods of measuring body composition

Whilst someone is alive all methods of measuring body composition are assessments based on research. There are numerous methods used in research, more advanced methods include MRI scanning. Less expensive methods include Bioelectrical Impedance that measures resistance of an electric current as it passes through the water content in the body, to then assess body fat from hydration.

One of the simplest and easiest methods to understand is skinfold.

Body fat percentage can be assessed by measuring the depth of a fold of skin at specific reference sites. Then comparing the results to researched reference tables a measure of body fat percentage can be achieved.

What is a skinfold caliper?

A skinfold caliper should allow you to measure the distance between the two "heads" of the gauge at a constant amount of pressure of 10 gms/mm2.
The caliper should have the following characteristics:
• Dial Graduation: 1 mm
• Measuring Range: 0 mm to 80 mm
• Measuring Pressure: 10 gms/mm2 (constant over range)

The elements of a human body

The human body is made up of numerous elements. It can be talked about in terms of chemical or anatomical elements. When talking about body fat, the relevant conversation is about the fat lying under the skin. Body fat should be considered partially as essential body fat. Some fat is stored around the body as packaging and stored where required and a large amount is stored under the surface of the skin as a form of insulation

With a weight management programme the two elements of the body that can change long term are fat mass and muscle mass. Using skinfold has the advantage of not measuring hydration, as water fluctuates considerably and skinfold directly measures adipose tissue.

The body fat stored under the skin in the subcutaneous layer is measured to provide a whole body fat calculation with skinfold calipers. The skin has a top skin layer, the epidermis and a middle layer, the dermis.

Fat	Adipose Tissue	Fat	Fat
		Essential Fat	
Protein	Muscle	Lean Body Mass	Lean Body Mass
CHO	Organs		
Water	Bone		
Mineral	Other		
Chemical Model	**Anatomical Model**	**Behnke 2 Part Model**	**Traditional 2 Part Model**

Essential Fat

- Makes up cell membranes and nerve fibres
- Provides up to 70% energy at rest
- Cushions vital organs
- Transports and stores fat-soluble vitamins
- Preserves body heat

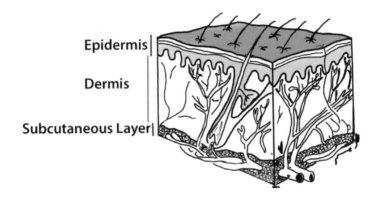

Epidermis

Dermis

Subcutaneous Layer

How to take a skinfold measurement

Skinfold data requires accurate measurements of skinfold readings. So some basic rules need to be applied to the method of taking readings.

Instruct the subject to keep relaxed during the test.

A skinfold measure is taken with the thumb and index finger, placing them on the skin about 10 cm apart and then pushing slightly down whilst gently sliding the  fingers together to "lift" a fold of skin.

The site of the reading and the size of the individual will mean dimensions may vary, but the principle of lifting a fold of skin proud is the essential concept.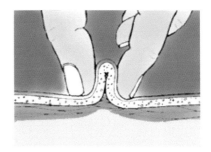

The caliper is then used to measure both the dermis and epidermis layers included with the fat contained in the subcutaneous layer. Once you have this fold of skin, keep the fold 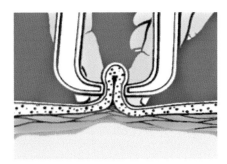 away from the skin and place the caliper next to the fingers to measure the fold. This reading should be taken in the first three seconds; before the skin is allowed to compress under the pressure of the caliper.

Then remove the caliper, release the skin and record the result.
The caliper should be perpendicular to the fold, approximately 1 cm below the finger and thumb. While maintaining hold of the skinfold, allow the caliper to be released so that full tension is placed on the skin.

Useful data

You will need to know the subject's gender, age and for a meaningful use of the data, body weight.

Also have a notepad handy to record skinfold readings.

Have a calculator to work out:

(Total weight / 100) x percentage of body fat   = fat weight

Total body weight - fat weight   =
lean weight

From the norm tables:

(Total weight / 100) x ideal percentage   = fat weight

Do this calculation to find the healthy fat weight range.

Check the BMI against the norm table to see if total body weight should be increasing or decreasing to be within the norms.

Site options

Once you know how to take a skinfold measurement you will have to compare your data to a reference table.

There are numerous options available from the ACSM (American College of Sports Medicine) , US Navy, etc. The two main references come from Jackson and Pollock in the USA and Durnin and Wormsley in Europe.

Jackson, A.S., Pollock, M.L. Generalized equations for predicting body density of men. British Journal of Nutrition. 40: 497–504, 1978.
Jackson, A.S., Pollock, M.L. and Ward A: Generalized equations for predicting body density of women. Med Sci Sports Exerc. 12: 175–182, 1980
Durnin and Womersley - British Journal of Nutrition / Volume32 / Issue01 / July 1974, pp 77-97

Durin & Wormsley – four site skinfold

With the Durin and Wormsley method the sum of four readings are added together and used with a gender-specific formula (or specific table).
The four sites are located as follows:

The right hand side of the body is generally used but consistency is the key.

See the video by going to https://youtu.be/VBJuVfiKrbY

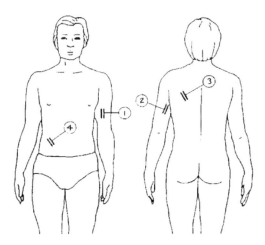

1/ Biceps

The anterior surface of the biceps midway between the anterior auxiliary fold and the antecubital fossa.

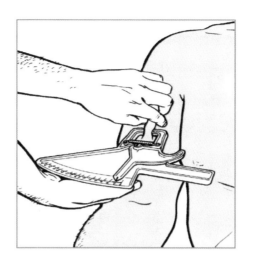

2/ Triceps

A vertical fold on the posterior midline of the upper arm, over the triceps muscle, halfway between the acromion process (bony process on top of the shoulder) and

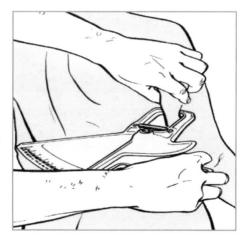

olecranon process (bony process on elbow). The elbow should be extended and the arm relaxed.

3/ Subscapular

The fold is taken on the diagonal line coming from the vertebral border to between 1 and 2 cm from the inferior angle of the scapula. (A diagonal fold about 1 to 2 cm below the point of the shoulder blade and 1 - 2 cm toward the arm.)

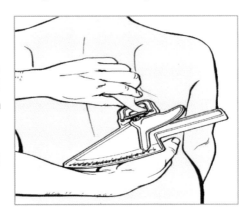

4/ Suprailiac

A diagonal fold above the crest of the ilium at the spot where an imaginary line would come down from the anterior auxiliary line just above the hip bone and 2 - 3 cm forward.

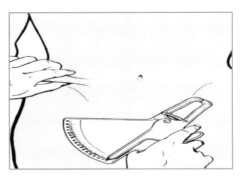

Calculation of body fat percentage

You can either:

• Use a formula on the internet:
  http://www.idass.com/bodyfatcalc/
• Use the Linear regression equation
• Use the look up tables

Linear regression equation

Body Density = C-[M (log 10 sum of all four skinfolds)]

MALE					
Age in years	17 – 19	20 – 29	30 – 39	40 – 49	50+
C	1.1620	1.1631	1.1422	1.1620	1.17515
M	0.0630	0.0632	0.0544	0.0700	0.0779

FEMALE					
Age in years	16 – 19	20 – 29	30 – 39	40 – 49	50+
C	1.1549	1.1599	1.1423	1.1333	1.1339
M	0.0678	0.0717	0.632	0.612	0.0645

Fat Percentage = [(4.95/Body Density)-4.5]x100

Skinfold calculation table

Male					Female				
	Age					Age			
Sum	17-20	30-39	40-49	50+	Sum	17-29	30-39	40-49	50+
15	4.8	8.00	8.29	8.60	15	10.5	14.7	15.9	17.8
20	8.1	12.2	12.2	12.5	20	14.1	17.0	19.8	21.4
22	9.2	13.0	13.4	13.9	22	15.4	18.0	20.0	22.6
24	10.2	13.8	14.4	15.1	24	16.5	18.9	21.2	23.7
26	11.2	14.6	15.5	16.3	26	17.6	19.9	22.3	24.8
28	12.1	15.4	16.6	17.4	28	18.6	20.8	23.4	25.7
30	12.9	16.2	17.7	18.6	30	19.5	21.8	24.5	26.6
35	14.7	17.7	19.8	20.8	35	21.6	23.7	26.4	28.6
40	16.4	19.2	21.4	22.9	40	23.4	25.5	28.2	30.3
45	17.7	20.4	23.0	24.7	45	25.0	26.9	29.6	31.9
50	19.0	21.5	24.6	26.5	50	26.5	28.2	31.0	33.4
55	20.1	22.5	25.9	27.9	55	27.8	29.4	32.1	34.6
60	21.2	23.5	27.1	29.2	60	29.1	30.6	33.2	35.7
65	22.2	24.3	28.2	30.4	65	30.2	31.6	34.1	36.7
70	23.1	25.1	29.3	31.6	70	31.2	32.5	35.0	37.7
75	24.0	25.9	30.3	32.7	75	32.2	33.4	35.9	38.7
80	24.8	26.6	31.2	33.8	80	33.1	34.3	36.7	39.6
85	25.5	27.2	32.1	34.8	85	34.0	35.1	37.5	40.4

90	26.2	27.8	33.0	35.8	90	34.8	35.8	38.3	41.2
95	26.9	28.4	33.7	36.6	95	35.6	36.5	39.0	41.9
100	27.6	29.0	34.4	37.4	100	36.4	37.2	39.7	42.6
110	28.8	30.1	35.8	39.0	110	37.8	38.6	41.0	43.9
120	30.0	31.1	37.0	40.1	120	39.0	39.6	42.0	45.1
130	31.0	31.9	38.2	41.8	130	40.2	40.6	43.0	46.2
140	32.0	32.7	39.2	40.3	140	41.3	41.6	44.0	47.2
150	32.9	33.5	40.2	44.1	150	42.3	42.6	45.0	48.2
160	33.7	34.3	41.2	45.1	160	43.3	43.6	45.8	49.2
170	34.5	34.8	42.0	46.1	170	44.1	44.4	46.6	50.0
180	35.3	35.4	42.7	47.0	180	45.0	45.2	47.4	50.8
190	35.9	35.9	43.5	47.9	190	45.8	45.9	48.2	51.6
200	36.5	36.7	44.5	48.8	200	46.5	46.5	48.8	52.4

18

Body Mass Index

With masses of data collected by health care professionals, a ratio of body weight to height has been calculated called "Body Mass index" or BMI that has provided data on a healthy weight in comparison to height.

You can use a simple slide rule to calculate BMI

or follow this simple formula.

BMI Body Mass Index = Weight (Kg) / Height (m) squared.

A BMI of between 20 – 25 for men and 20 - 30 for women is considered to be healthy.

BMI does not take into account the component model of the human body, where body mass is made up of fat mass, muscle mass, hydrated water mass etc.

Ensure you have an accurate reading for height and weight, often these readings are falsely reported if you just ask.
Body weight should be taken without shoes, heavy clothes or items in pockets etc. and not after a large meal.
Consistency in readings from measurement to measurement is key.

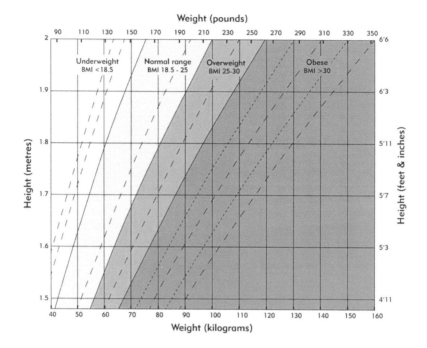

Weight (pounds)

Underweight
BMI <18.5

Normal range
BMI 18.5 - 25

Overweight
BMI 25-30

Obese
BMI >30

Height (metres)

Height (feet & inches)

Weight (kilograms)

21

Normal values of body fat

Once you have a reading of body fat percentage it is just a numerical value. The categorisation of values of body fat have been carried out by the World Health Organisation (WHO). The values are best expressed in the following table.

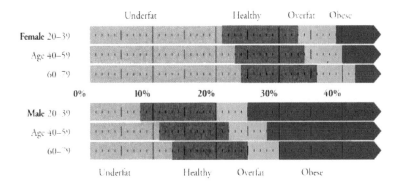

22

Results Calculations Table

	Value
Bicep skinfold	mm
Tricep skinfold	mm
Sub Scapular skinfold	mm
Supra Iliac skinfold	mm
Total skinfold	mm
Body fat percentage	%
Body weight	Kg
Body weight / 100	1%
Percent body weight x fat % = fat weight	Kg
Total weight – fat weight = lean weight	Kg
Ideal fat percentage	%

Current fat percentage +/- ideal percentage	% change
Current weight +/- % change = target fat weight change	Kg
100 - ideal fat percentage = Ideal lean percentage	%
Total body weight x ideal lean percentage = Target lean weight estimate*	Kg

Target lean weight is hard to calculate using this simple table as the total body weight may or may not currently be an ideal. So to state the lean weight is ideal is based on the current bodyweight being ideal.

Calculating useful values

Having measured a subject's body fat percentage, two simple questions should be considered. Does the subject have

1. A healthy body fat percentage?
    i.e. should they try to lose fat?

2. A healthy body mass index?
    i.e. should they either lose fat or increase muscle mass to achieve the ideal body mass?

Basal Metabolic Rate

The rate at which the body uses energy while at rest to maintain vital functions such as breathing and keeping warm.

you can use the formula below to calculate basal (resting) metabolic rate.

$$BMR = [99.8 + 1.155 (Wt) + 0.02227 (60 \times Lean\ Wt) - 0.4563 (Age)] \times 7.2$$

Where BMR = Kcal / day.

Or go to the internet on the Bodyfatcal page on the www.idass.com website

A simple weight loss guide

It is a very simple rule that there are 500 calories in a pound of fat.
There are 2.2 pounds in a kilo.
So if a 500 calorie deficit in the diet was achieved a pound of fat loss.

It may be a simple rule but often the simple ones provide an easy to understand solid basis. Only in very extreme cases can weight loss not be achieved by reducing calorie intake.

People struggling to lose weight often are not aware of how many calories they are consuming, they forget or do not realise. e.g. Drinking alcohol or sugar laden drinks, full fat milk

If the diet is becoming a bit blurred around the edges, then a simple nutrition log of what is eaten on a spot day or week, is often revealing.

Nutrition Log / Diary

Name:

Date:

	Meal	Protein	Carbs	Fat
BREAKFAST				
SNACK				
LUNCH				

SNACK				
DINNER				
	TOTAL			

28

Dictionary

accuracy

noun
the quality or state of being correct or precise.
the degree to which the result of a measurement, calculation, or specification conforms to the correct value or a standard.

basal metabolic rate

noun: **basal metabolic rate**; plural noun: **basal metabolic rates**
the rate at which the body uses energy while at rest to maintain vital functions such as breathing and keeping warm.

caliper

noun
an instrument for measuring external or internal dimensions, having two hinged legs resembling a pair of compasses and in-turned or out-turned points.

dermis

noun : **dermis**
the skin.
the thick layer of living tissue below the epidermis which forms the true skin, containing blood capillaries, nerve endings, sweat glands, hair follicles, and other structures.

epidermis

noun: **epidermis**; plural noun: **epidermises**
the surface epithelium of the skin, overlying the dermis.

fat

noun: **fat**; plural noun: **fats**
a natural oily substance occurring in animal bodies,
especially when deposited as a layer under the skin or
around certain organs.

ideal

adjective: **ideal**
satisfying one's conception of what is perfect; most
suitable.

percentage

noun: **percentage**; plural noun: **percentages**
a rate, number, or amount in each hundred, proportion
or share in relation to a whole.

quality

noun
the standard of something as measured against other
things of a similar kind; the degree of excellence of
something.

ratio

noun: **ratio**; plural noun: **ratios**
the quantitative relation between two amounts showing the number of times one value contains or is contained within the other.

skinfold

noun: **skinfold**; plural noun: **skinfolds**;
a fold of skin and underlying fat formed by pinching, the thickness of which is a measure of nutritional status.

truth

noun: **truth**
the quality or state of being true. that which is true or in accordance with fact or reality.

Conversion Data Metric Imperial

To convert	into	Multiply by
Centimetres	Inches	0.394
Inches	Centimetres	2.54
Kilograms	Pounds	2.205
Pound	Kilograms	0.454
Kilocalories (KCal)	kilojoules	4.184 (kJ)

Printed in Great Britain
by Amazon

45900658R00021